Amit Kainth

THE GIFT

7 LAWS OF SUCCESS

AUSTIN MACAULEY
PUBLISHERS LTD.

A CIP catalogue record for this title is available from the British Library.

ISBN 978 1 84963 767 1

www.austinmacauley.com

First Published (2014)
Austin Macauley Publishers Ltd.
25 Canada Square
Canary Wharf
London
E14 5LB

Printed and bound in Great Britain

God has given you life on earth which is a Gift. He wants you to live your life by these 7 laws and in return you will become **The Gift** to God.

Read this book carefully. Take your time and don't rush it because all your answers lie within.

Introduction

This book is written for everyone and anyone, regardless of your culture, religion, beliefs, skin colour, age, gender, sexual orientation, occupation, the list goes on. This is not a religious book, but a spiritual one. 'The Gift' is a set of 7 laws, all with a transcendent foundation, that once understood and used together in daily life situations, will take us to where we want to be. It is important to pin point the fact that these laws are stripped of any religious connotation. I am not here to defend religious perspectives or say that a particular religion is better than the other, or even a particular culture has better rules than the rest. I am here to teach that no matter what religion you have, what culture you come from, or what beliefs you may believe in; there is a common power source to all of us that many have experienced, others question, and a few refuse altogether. To excel and be successful in any areas of our lives, whether in love relationships, work/business, family dynamics, etc.; we will have to open our eyes to what happens around us on a daily basis, and understand that there is something very powerful above our 'simple' human dimension that leads the way and forms our destiny – this power source, divine power, energy, God, Father, Lord; whatever name you want to give it, is behind you and inside you, and it rules interactions among people, animals, nature and every living thing on earth.

Even sceptical people can understand, accept and use The Gift; the secret is to have patience and an open mind to new ideas and concepts that may challenge your usual way of seeing reality. Science nowadays can pretty much explain anything and everything, and the fact that God cannot be seen, explained, pinpointed, recorded, etc., may raise questions and doubts among many. Scientists have studied many aspects of our planet, our solar system, and ultimately, with the tools that are available, our Universe. We have theories on how everything has been created – such as the Big Bang theory,

Darwin's theory of evolution, etc. We also have evidence of what we are made of – atoms, molecules, cells, etc. We even have sciences that tell us how nature interacts and works within itself (mathematics, physics, biology…); and subjective ones like neurology and psychology that explain why we act in certain ways. Regardless of what science it is, there are still questions that remain unanswered. Like I said, I am not here to say who is right, who is wrong, or if there is any right or wrong answer; I am here to open your eyes to the unanswered.

One of the most debated subjects amongst scholars since history began is the matter of consciousness. We have studied how our brain works, and even how our emotions affect the way we think and act. But no one has ever been able to explain why we are beings with a conscious. What is consciousness? It is generally accepted as truth that there is an extra element to our human form that goes beyond our brain and our body – some may call this consciousness, others call it Soul. The fact is that we all have one, although where it came from and who created it is still a mystery.

When you feel that something is missing in your life; when you feel you could do better, when you feel you just can't get there alone; when you feel it is impossible, this is the time that you should look for answers, you should research, look around you, analyse what is there, and what isn't. This is the time that you should seek the truth about the Power. However, the problem with us is that we only call on this power when we need help, and it does not always work this way. We need to constantly lean on the power throughout our life and build a full on relationship with the divine.

Our relationship with the Power should be like someone in the marines. There is a saying among soldiers to always look after the person next to you and not break their trust; in return, they will look after you and not break your trust. In order to really excel in this life we need the power behind us, and in order to have it fully behind us, one needs to live according to these 7 laws. Once you live within these 7 Laws you will be experiencing a different life, which is controlled by the power. However, this is your choice, you can chose to have it behind you or you can choose to live a life without it, ultimately the decision lies in your hands.

If you believe that there is no divine power beyond these worlds that created the universe then research and read about it. Read about science, religion, beliefs. Read about those who had near death experiences. They will describe to you what they have seen and what they were confronted by when they saw beyond the curtain to the other side. These experiences tell us what happens to our consciousness or Soul, where it goes, what happens to it once our time on earth comes to an end. However, no matter how many people you speak to, if you do not experience life with the Power behind it, you will never be satisfied and will always live in denial. It's like driving a car – until you get into the driving seat yourself, you will never experience how it feels to manoeuvre a vehicle. The same principle applies here; we must want to know this Power. We must want to experience Him, and see with our own eyes what He gives us; we must sit in the driver's seat in life, and experience the full power of God on a daily basis.

This is the first step to succeed in life – to open our eyes to every possibility. Being open minded is the only way we will be able to see, absorb and analyse what happens around us, and eventually act upon it in the right way. Albert Einstein once said "I don't try to imagine a personal God; it suffices to stand in awe at the structure of the world, insofar as it allows our inadequate senses to appreciate it". Look around you, look at how perfect our world is, how perfect our bodies are, how perfectly arranged is nature. Like Einstein said, it is sufficient to stare around us in amazement and see how everything interacts together, and understand that we, human beings, are only a minimal fraction on earth, on our solar system, on our universe, and our senses are inadequate to understand anything that goes beyond our daily reality. Nevertheless, if you don't want to try and imagine a power force or a God per say – look around you, that is sufficient. Only then can one use The Gift – the 7 laws that will bring you success, contentment and peace.

This book is firmly founded on the concept of Karma. Everyone has come across this concept at some stage in their lives. The saying "what goes around, comes around" is widely known across the world, and all of us have experienced Karma in some way. When we lie, cheat, hurt, etc., we know we are setting a chain of negative actions that will eventually come back to us. If we are jealous, mean and deceitful to anyone around us, it will only bring back headache – people to whom you act negatively upon, will definitely not turn around and be nice to you. Similarly, they will go to others and speak wrong of you. Or they may take actions into their own hands to hurt you back. We all know that if you are unfair and do something bad to someone, it will eventually catch up with us. A classic example is lying. When you lie to someone, even if that person does not know the truth, you will have to hide, create more lies to cover the initial lie, which can quickly turn into a snowball effect so big that you realise it is getting out of control and you are in real trouble. Karmic laws are always running around us. Not only with negative actions, but with positive ones too. If we help one another, say compliments, being friendly, etc., the chances of people having the same positive attitude towards us are very high. This can put us in front of good opportunities; challenges that will make us strong, networks of people that can help us, etc. Karma is everywhere around us, and we can see it daily, in any situation, with any person.

Everyone has a Karmic balance, and it is important to have an eye on this karmic balance in order to keep it positive. If we are horrible people who kill, hurt and deceive; the number of people who will be after us, or trying to hurt us back, etc. will be enormous and we will constantly be running into bad situations and bad things will happen to us – our karmic balance will be negative. Conversely, if we are good people, are positive towards others, friendly, helpful, loving and caring; the interactions with others will be so positive that we will constantly be faced with good opportunities, kind words from people, good treatment and the same love and care back – our karmic balance is positive. We should always have our karmic balance in mind, even though we get caught in our busy stressful lives, we need to always be looking at our karma. Look at it like a football match – even though you have the teams, the ball, the defence, the attack and all these elements to be worrying about while the game goes on; every player has the goal net in the back of their minds; to score the goal is the ultimate objective and it is what actually rules the game. Karma is what rules our game of life, and wanting to have a positive Karma is essential to be able to understand The Gift, use it, and succeed with it.

Now, not only does karma exist around you, it also determines a lot of what happens to you. Not only on an hourly basis, but on a daily basis, by the week, month, and yearly basis. If we do something really wrong in our jobs today, like stealing money, eventually this will be discovered, and if it is, you might lose your job. Essentially, an action that you do today may have repercussions for the next couple of years of your life. It is safe to say that we make our own destiny in a sense, we are the judges of how our lives develop, and our actions are behind all of this. However, there are set things in our lives that we have no control over; for instance, your family – you did not choose your family, and the way you were brought up can shape how you see the world and how you live your life. You cannot control your health either. We know we can hurt our body with drugs, alcohol, etc. and if we are not careful we can contract certain diseases, but ultimately, the tendency for one to have cancer, or dementia, Alzheimer's, heart problems, asthma, and so on; is under no one's control. We all have a destiny, a destiny set by God that we are meant to reach through our own free will. The actions and decisions we take throughout our lives will decide when, where and how we reach our destiny. The Gift will help you minimize the time to reach your destiny, advise you on how to reach it, and keep your mind and soul on the right path.

The Gift consists of 7 laws. These, if followed thoroughly, will realise your full potential as a human being, as a conscious being. The 7 laws are: *Meditation; Give God the Glory; Flow; Transparency; Minimize Outward Negative Actions; Stay around Positive Souls* and *To be Pure of Heart*. These laws are all directly connected to God, to us, and to our surroundings. In this book I will introduce, explain and explore each of the laws, guiding you through them – the overall objective is for you to change your perspective of the world, of yourself and of God – in the end you will start seeing the results in your life. I will refer to God as a person in many instances, but it is at one's discretion to understand what God is, a power, a divine being, or any other perspective or interpretation. God in this book is the one who created us and who has given us the opportunity to go through this amazing test to our souls – Life.

However the choice is yours, no one will force you, or drag you there, it is something you have to do yourself. By choosing not to access the divine power or choosing to ignore it or not work with it, no one will lose out but you. Find out what is actually going on; get closer to the truth, use the Gift, and you will see – it will take you beyond your imagination.

The success you have in life does not depend on how many hours you spend in the office or how many hours you spend with loved ones. Your success will be driven depending on how many hours you spend on these laws. The more time spent on 'The Gift', the more contentment, successful relationships, love, peace, happiness and wealth you will have in return.

About Me

My parents came from Africa when they were young and settled in the Midlands. My family always had businesses running and my dad, a great man, always managed to provide me, my mother and my older brother with many opportunities to grow strong and lead a successful life. We used to go to the temple on a regular basis. I never thought too deeply about what going to the temple meant, it was more a part of our lives and culture than a meaningful ritual. I never explored the concept of God, and never really thought about it or related it to my life.

My career began at the age of 21 in banking, and I worked my way up within two years to become a financial adviser. The money was never good enough so I made the decision to go into business. After spending several months researching the market, I bought a franchise in recruitment. Borrowing the money from my parents to set the business up, very quickly I became successful and soon we had contracts with Banks and building societies providing top calibre individuals. In a short period of time I bought myself a brand new Porsche and by the age of 25 I was driving an Aston Martin. With the money the company was making I started to invest it wisely in other ventures. Before I knew it, I was the owner of various businesses ranging from bars, restaurant to various retail outlets, including a hair salon and discount stores. I was feeling high on all the success, greedy for more money, more cars and more businesses. I have always been competitive by nature, everything is a game for me, or a bet, or something to win. I always put 150% into what I want, sometimes not looking at means to reach ends.

In May 2009, before I hit 30 years old, I lost it all. What took me several years to build, I lost within months. The empire came crashing down and there was nothing I could do to sustain the businesses. We lost clients for no apparent reasons, managing to close deals became a struggle. To keep the recruitment business going I sold my shares from a bar I owned to a friend, however, it was not enough. I tried everything in my power to keep the companies going and to sustain the businesses, but nothing I did was good enough.

Eventually all the businesses collapsed, all the properties defaulted, and to hit me even harder, later that same year I had to declare myself bankrupt. I was finished, the game was over.

All I had was my brave wife, who had stood by me through the great, the good, the bad and the worst times. She gave birth to our gorgeous son in the same year that I lost everything. I did not have a penny to my name, my empire was lost, and I had a little boy to raise, educate and support.

I remember when I went bankrupt, I had a very intense meeting with the administrators, who interrogated me for 3 hours and thought I had committed fraud and demanded answers as to how I could go bankrupt, under the light of years of successful business. Even the receiver could not believe it, but I was broke, miserable, depressed and most importantly had no answers or explanations as to how this all happened.

The alcohol and prescription drugs that were part of my life during those years of success quickly took over my depressed self and within months I was admitted to hospital. For a period of time no one knew what was wrong with me and I nearly lost my life. I had hit rock bottom and I just could not see myself getting out of this situation. I had a form of internal bleeding in my digestive tract, mainly my stomach, that became so aggravated that I was at risk of dying. I was completely helpless, with no money and no health. I was finished and I can remember thinking to myself that I might as well be dead as I have very little to go back to. At that time I did not believe in anything but myself, when I had all the money I thought it was me doing it all and little was wrong.

However, the thought of my family, my wife, my new-born son made me hold on to life. Now that I look back, it was the only thing that made me fight through the depression and not give up. Whilst in hospital, I began to pray. I did not believe in God per say, as I mentioned before, it was always a part of my life but a very superficial one. I did not know who I was speaking to when I prayed, or what I would get out of doing this but I had nothing else to give me hope.

One night, after endless exams and tests, the medical staff came into my room and began to take me out towards the operating theatre. I pleaded with them not to take me to surgery but they wouldn't listen. I begged them to stop but they repeatedly informed me that if I didn't get operated on, the chances of living through the night were decreasing by the minute. After a lot of debating and arguing, they agreed to give me until the morning before performing the surgery, as this operation would have changed my life radically in terms of aptitude to work, or even ability to carry on a 'normal' life. I would most probably be impaired if I survived the operation. I asked the doctors and pleaded to let me be me until the next morning – if they still needed to do the operation by then, I would give my consent.

That night I don't know who I was asking, or what I was praying for. All I knew was that I wanted to get out of this situation and I asked over and over again for help, throughout the night. The next morning my medical consultant sent me for pre-surgery scans to see my internal condition and assess the damage that I had suffered by refusing to be operated on the night before. When they got the scan results back, they were shocked to see that I was fine. It was a complete miracle, no one could believe it and there was no need to operate on me. I was not cured, but the aggravated condition I was in the night before that made everyone, doctors and family, fear for my life was not evident anymore. I was put on a high dosage of prescribed drugs and antibiotics, but within a few weeks I was discharged and I was given a second chance.

Once I came out of hospital I had a lot of time on my hands while recovering. I had no work or business to be attached to, and I was at home all the time making sure I would not fall ill again, as my condition was still fragile. I began to question what had just happened. Why was I so wealthy in the first place and why did I lose it all? Who has been in control of my life so far that gave me everything I thought I wanted and then took everything away from me? Why did I nearly lose my life and why was I saved? Who saved me? I was so confused by all the occurrences of the last months that I needed to re-focus.

I wanted and demanded answers. I started to read a lot of spiritual and religious books and I found there were many of the same elements present in all of them. Heaven was one element, evil too, souls, energy, God – all of these were described and mentioned over and over again in different religions from around the world. There were other characteristics that were also practiced by many, which although were done in different ways, all had the same core laws and rules. An example of this was meditation. I read about meditation in Buddhism. I began to meditate, trying to blank my mind and elevate that consciousness, that soul to connect with God. Whilst meditating, several messages came to me so I wrote them down. After a couple of years I found that I had over 100 of these messages noted. Someone was inspired by the work and made a small book called "*100 quotes of God*". Today I give this book to places that need it, like hospitals, hospices, homeless, charities and various local churches, in an attempt to give people in need some hope.

After a while I went further, deeper into meditation and then I came up with THE GIFT. This is a set of rules that I have used over the last couple of years and have given me peace, contentment, successful relationships and wealth. Today my wealth is eight times what it was before I lost everything and went to hospital. This wealth has been achieved in a third of the time it took me previously. All because I stopped, looked around, opened my eyes and eventually my heart, and listened to God. Once I did this, I was able to see clearly what God wanted me to see, a set of logical laws that if followed will give you true happiness rather than a fake temporary happiness fabricated by money and material goods. THE GIFT is God's gift to me, and I would like to share it with you. I hope you enjoy it and that it helps you in your life as much as it did in mine.

Chapter 1

Meditation (The Five Negative Forces)

"For him who has conquered the mind, the mind is the best friend of friends, but for one who has failed to do so, his mind will remain the greatest enemy."

(Bhagavad Gita 6.6)

There are five negative forces which are always pulling us down. These are Greed, Pride, Lust, Anger and Attachment. If you look and analyse your day today, there will be at least one of these elements that brought you down, depending on the circumstances you were in.

The mind is designed to be drawn to these five elements. These elements are our weaknesses and can actually destroy us.

I want you to think back to the last time you made a bad decision, and I can guarantee that one of the five forces, Greed Pride, Lust, Anger or Attachment had something to do with it. Every day we have choices and free will to make the right or wrong decision, and every time we make an awful decision it sets us back in life and drives us away from our goals. This chapter/element shows us how to deactivate the five evil forces, enabling us to make the right decisions in life so we can climb to our greatest heights.

We need to deactivate these forces, or, if you like, make them weaker. We do this through meditation. When we meditate we are powering down the five forces and minimising them, allowing us to make the correct decisions so we are able to excel.

The reason we are in this state is because our minds are very strong and we fuel them all the time, in business, work, men, women, attachment to cars, houses etc....so every day the mind gets better and stronger. When we meditate, we are fuelling the soul. The overall objective is to make the soul so powerful it overrides the mind.

The mind will say go left but the soul will want you to go right. The soul is the energy source that always wants to do the right thing, but we always listen to the mind because it is led by the five negative forces overriding the soul.

We need to get to a position where we are listening to our soul. In order to make the soul stronger we need to meditate and awaken it.

For example, take an instance whereby a shopkeeper has given you £10 note rather than a £5 note by mistake. Your mind says that you can use the extra money, but deep down you know that is not the right thing to do. If you return the money then you know your soul is stronger than your mind. However, if you say that it is the shopkeeper's negligence and you keep the extra cash, then your mind is very powerful and overrides the soul. This is Greed.

Another example, if you are married and another man or woman asks you out for a drink, and you say yes, you know it is the wrong thing to do, but you enjoy that person and you continue the plan to go out. It means that the mind is being stronger than the soul. This is Lust.

Or if you have a business and you are putting all possible time into it. You know it is the wrong thing to do, because you should be spending more time with your partner or kids, but due to the mind getting attached to earthly things (cars, houses, businesses, etc.), it is something you cannot help yourself from doing. This is Attachment.

When you come home from a hard day at work, grumpy because the day did not go your way, you will be angry and project that on your family. You know deep down it is not their fault but because the mind is so strong it cannot help itself from shouting at those closest to you. This is Anger.

Then once you have shouted, you should instantly go and apologise, but you can't do it. Your mind is so powerful and full of pride. This negative force is the ego that stops us loving one another to our full potential.

The reason we behave this way is because our minds are very active and resilient. We need a way of shutting the mind down and deactivating it. You might think that your mind goes to sleep at night, but even when you are asleep the five elements are active. Think about what you were doing in your last dream. I can guarantee you one of the five elements were active.

So the only way we can deactivate these five elements is by meditating. There are many different forms of meditation you can do. For example, one form of meditation is repetition of a word or reciting the same prayer over and over again. The repetition of a word powers down the mind and eventually blanks it. Another form of meditation is silent meditation, where you just sit in a quiet corner and try to blank your mind in silence. A third form of meditation is listening to relaxing music and letting your mind clear up under the sound of the melody. There is a lot of meditation music available and you can simply Google them, obtain them from book stores or even on YouTube. You will find this helps to shut down the five forces. Lastly, there are walking and guided meditations which are usually carried out with an instructor talking you through the whole process. Everywhere there are courses or sessions that you can join and learn to meditate; ask around and get informed, you will be surprised how it will make you feel after a couple of tries. The more we meditate and practice the better we become at deactivating the mind and powering down the five forces. This does sound harsh but if you currently evaluate your life, you may find that you are a prisoner of these five forces. Most people are not in control of them, but are instead controlled by them. The overall objective is to try to practice meditation every day. One day in your life you are going to be in a situation where you will be able to weaken or even turn off the five elements when faced with difficult situations. This will allow you to become stronger and able to fight when you hit a downturn; whether you lose your job, a loved one passes away, you are going through disturbance in your marriage, a divorce or even trouble with your kids.

Meditation is like any form of exercise. You have to practice. It does not come overnight, but takes years of dedication. It's like learning to drive; it takes time, and requires lessons with great focus, dedication and determination.

Meditation should not be practiced because you need to, or because you have been told to do so. This form of exercise is your communication link between you and the divine power, the creator of the universe. The weaker the meditation, the weaker the relationship; the stronger the meditation, the stronger the connection will be. This exercise should not be taken lightly. It should be kept in first place in your life and should be carried out with full heart and soul. The more time and effort spent in meditation the better the link becomes between you and the divine source.

One of the purposes of meditation is to obtain direction and there should be a point in meditation where you are silent, allowing the answers to come through, directing and guiding you to make the right decisions. This form of exercise can be done sitting on the floor, on the couch, on the bed or a chair. However, the most important thing is to lie still because when we are in this state we are able to connect to the divine power, and your body becomes an irrelevant element.

By repeating one word or words, the mind will be calm and relaxed, playing down the five forces. You could repeat brick, brick, brick over and over; or stone, stone, stone. The word chosen is irrelevant. It is the exercise that is important. However, in most cases the word or words that people often use are of a spiritual nature, as this can bring quicker results in attempting to clear and blank your mind. My advice is if you don't know how, then go today and find someone who can teach you the art of meditation and you will see by putting it into practice, over time you will become a better and, consequently, more successful person.

But please do not expect results overnight or even in two or three months. It takes an average person six months to learn how to drive and pass their test. Be patient and do not feel demotivated as it can take a considerable amount of time. The important thing is that you keep at it and you sit down in the same place at the same time every day and practice.

Our minds are designed to want more wealth, women/men, houses, cars and other material possessions. However, if you think about it, what are you asking for? You are asking for the five downward forces, greed, pride, lust, attachment and anger. The only way to find peace is to get the soul to override the mind. The only way to do this is through meditation. This is when success, happiness and peace come into play.

To become a successful person in business, work or personal life you need to make decisions without the five forces active. You cannot become attached to the business, or make decisions with anger, or employ someone with lust or sit down with someone with pride, or operate unethically letting greed get in the way.

In a lot of successful businesses you don't see the owner around because he/she is operating it without attachment. In order to realise the full potential of the gift we need to meditate and weaken the five forces. Then we will learn to make decisions in life without attachment, lust, greed, anger and pride.

People often ask me how much time we should spend in meditation. The honest answer is: there are no time limits, but do it until your heart is content and always put it first before any worldly activities. However, the more time you spend in meditation, the more time you are trying to have a relationship with that divine power/God/Father. Now if you believe in the saying "what you sow is what you shall reap", then because you are sewing good positive actions towards the divine then you will begin to reap the benefits. For example, you will see that you get that lucky break, it will put the right people in front of you, it will give you the right relationships, it will give you the right opportunity, and you will not need to go looking for it – your desires and outcomes will automatically come to you.

Meditation is so important that it is labelled the first element in this book. You should now also put meditation first place in your life and in return you will then see that the divine power will take control over your destiny and elevate you to heights with minimal effort from yourself.

Believe it or not, when you do any form of meditation or prayer you attract the higher energy/angels/God towards you. The problem with us is that we meditate or pray with full heart and soul only when we are going through a tough time in life. If you do this form of exercise when you are high in your life, you will see what you can achieve. Without the five forces commanding your actions, you will be spreading positive attitude, thoughts and words that will help others and will spread so wide in the world that they will come back to you. Great things will present themselves, taking you to high altitudes, whether it is in your work, love life, business, family life, etc. Change your life, action this from this moment, and make your life better for you and your family.

This will be a difficult transition. The reason being that since you were born you have constantly been pulled by these five forces. The mind does not like change and now you are asking it to do something that goes against the tide. This is not an easy task but with practice it can be mastered. Eventually you will come to discover that there is no need to chase worldly activities because once you put meditation first the worldly activities just come to you naturally.

Chapter 2

Give God the Glory

The relationship we have with God should be one of truth and only truth. The relationship with God should be one of give and take, trusting him to guide you through good and bad. The best way to live your life is to delegate to God and then to trust Him with whatever outcome that arrives. If you feel you are not satisfied with the result then you must learn not to question His work as He who is in charge knows the greater plan. We are merely dust particles in this universe and who are we to question the divine that brought us here in the first place? Be grateful that it is because of the divine you are here and never forget where you come from. Remember we are here on loan, only temporarily we stand here on earth, and soon we will be back with the power, the creator of the universe.

When you are working for a company as an employee you go to your manager or boss for direction and you report to them, follow their instructions and do as you are told. Failure to do so means you can lose the relationship and as a result you will find being at work a daunting task. This is the same way we should treat our relationship with the divine: listen to your inner voice, your soul, and follow His direction in what we should be doing in our lives. God is the one that should be directing us like an employee. Here we are leading two lives: one of the worldly pursuits and the other led by our father. Lead a balanced life and don't neglect either one of them as they are both equally important.

The best way to describe this is: you have to trust God 100% and not half heartedly. For example: you say to God, "I really want to buy a house." Then you apply for a mortgage and once you have your finances in place, you start to search the market for the right property. You find the right property and put an offer in. Weeks later you find out that the property sale has fallen through, and get disappointed and upset. You start to blame God – "why didn't we get the property?" This is where people fall down and start to lose faith. The mind has gotten attached to the property. What we should do in this situation is to thank God for not allowing us to buy this property and say we wait for you to find another one. Accept God's decision gracefully rather than getting upset or blaming God. God never says no, He only says yes, not yet or I have something better for you.

Another example: you apply for a job and you pray that you get it. You go for a 2 or 3 stage interview and you get rejected. You lose faith and start to blame God – "why didn't I get the job?" We don't know why God did not give us the job and if we don't know why, then we should not question his work.

We have to devote ourselves to God, put him first and trust him in all outcomes. Once you put all your trust in God and have devoted your life to him, then you know he is in charge and in the driving seat. Whatever outcome arises, accept and embrace it, as only he knows your greater plan, and understands the best solution for you. Remember who actually analyses whether the situation is good or bad. The mind does, which is driven by the five forces. You might think that the situation is bad but really all that happened is the mind got attached (attachment is one of the negative five forces that constantly pull us down) to the house, the job or the car we did not get. That is all. So ask yourself if the situation is really bad or if God saved you for something better.

I cannot express this any further. We need to trust God completely 100% and thank him for everything that comes our way, no matter how the mind interprets it, good or bad. Always thank God and put God first.

Now, I know it might be difficult to keep faith in the divine when you are going through a tough time but it is especially when you are being tested that you should still keep faith. You won't just be tested once, but again and again and it is at this time you are most vulnerable and can lose your balance. You then have to lean on the power 150% because the divine will get you out of bad situations. You always need to keep relying on it no matter what. The secret behind breaking this cycle and excelling to a higher level is to constantly lean on the power throughout both the tough times and the good times, and not when you feel or choose to.

An example of what our relationship with God should be is like one of a mother or father with their child. Imagine you give birth to a child, bring them up and devote your whole life to giving them the best. Then one day they turn their back and decide that they don't need to rely on you and start to venture into the big wide world. How would you feel? You would feel let down, hurt and disappointed. However if the child decides to return and come back you would welcome them with open arms.

This is the exact relationship we have with God; he is always trying to reunite us with him but we don't listen or we only listen when we want to. When we want him he is always there and welcomes us with open arms. However, to realise his full potential we need to have absolute faith. Similarly, if your parents think we come back to them and they feel we will go again, they will not give all their love as they feel they might get hurt again.

God is the same. He will only unleash his full power with fully devoted people and to the ones he knows will not turn against him, no matter how much or how little he gives away.

Let's say, for example, you have children and one child tends not to appreciate or acknowledge that you buy them things with your hard earned cash. Later in life, because it is your child and you love them, you then give a bigger gift, but again it doesn't get acknowledged, and he/she doesn't say 'thank you'. Again later in life, because your love is so strong for that child you keep giving gifts, but he/she doesn't show any sign of love back, or appreciation. Because there is no love back, you will give more to your other children as they show appreciation. With the spoilt child, you are careful with what you give because there is no love or gratitude back. You don't release the full potential that you can actually give, so you hold back. This is the same in relationships with God. If you are not grateful and thankful for what he has already given, and appreciate the position you are in now and you don't thank him on a daily basis, then God will also hold back what He can actually give you. Instead He will just provide you what you need to get by.

We need to get into the habit of thanking God all the time and in all the events that happen in our life, throughout the hour, throughout the day and throughout the years to come and not just when we choose to. We normally just remember God on Sundays when we go to the church or temple. Or we thank God before dinner and say grace. Or we remember God when we feel low. We should not live life in this way, but to give God the glory in all aspects of our life. This law is so powerful that it states it in so many places in the bible: Thessalonians 5:16-18: "Be joyful; pray continually; give thanks in all circumstances for this is God's will".

A classic example is if a business is going well, and someone says to you, "wow, you're doing well. How you are doing it?" Nine times out of ten, your pride hits the roof and you then start boasting about the number of employees you hire, the sales you have achieved, the car you are driving and automatically you start to feel above everyone else. For one moment in that conversation, do you stop to say, "actually, God gave me all this?" We should be saying, "God has given me all this and it is thanks to Him I am in this position." To change our lives and to get the full abundance and love from God we need to give God the full glory. Speak it and tell others when they ask you in conversation.

Sometimes in life things go badly but suddenly it turns out to be a good result, we say an expression "thank God for that". However, we say this without meaning it and it is just an expression. When we thank God we have to stop and think, say it with meaning and it has to come from the heart. Psalm 105:1-2: "Give thanks to the Lord, call on his name; make known among his nations what he has done. Sing to him, sing praise to him, and tell of all his wonderful acts."

We have to choose and accept that God is the provider and include him in our daily lives and not when we choose to bring him in. When we want something in life and in conversation, we should say, "God willing I will see you tomorrow," or, "God willing we will buy a house next year," or, "God willing we will buy a car." We need to get in the habit of inviting God into our lives, dropping our pride and accepting that He is in control of our destiny.

Many successful people have adopted this policy already. They are open about it and thank God out loud. However, some are not so open and will say it inside when they have a quiet moment. The truth of the matter is that this element needs to be adopted and brought into our lives, and if we are not already doing so, then start from today, give God the glory for everything that happens in our daily life and thank him for all that happens.

We have to realise that we were made out of love. The power of the divine is all love and there is no hate in the relationship with God. Please don't get confused. Things that happen to us are a product of Karmic laws rather than a product of the relationship one should have with God. These are two different things. God created this world fairly for all and that's why the karmic laws exist. So if you ask yourself why God is doing bad things to you, God is NOT. The bad things that happen to you are your own doings, either from this life or a past one. God is all love and you were created out of love. He will always forgive what you have done. The karmic law is there to make life fair for all creatures. If we have done bad things then one day we will pay for them, the same way if we have done good things then one day we will reap the rewards. God does not judge us for what we have done. God just wants you to turn your head towards him, to change your life, to work towards the GIFT so you can reach the true heights of what you were sent here on earth to do.

The problem with us all is that we find this element hard to adopt because we feel that we have sinned too much to start a relationship with God. Forget the past and what has happened because that cannot be changed. You must now look forward and treat people how you would like to be treated and plant seeds on the rewards you want to receive. It is impossible to live on this earth without sinning. Everyone has sinned. Everyone has done bad things, everyone has ill commented on others, everyone has cheated in life and no one is perfect. We all fall short in the Glory of God. God does not care how much you have sinned because the karmic law takes care of that. Now remember what happens to you today is a result of your own previous actions. So no one is to blame but yourself and you should go through this smilingly. God just wants you to turn your heads towards him and to start appreciating what he has given you, to draw a line under everything and start a new beginning today. Psalm 106:1: "Praise the Lord. Give thanks to the Lord, for he is good; his love endures forever."

The only thing that God wants is for you to remember him whilst on earth and to appreciate what he has given to you. Life here on earth is short and he wants you to live and enjoy your life, as this opportunity may not come again. He has brought you down to earth to do good things for humanity and to change others' lives. God is the true master and you should live your life for him, keeping him in the forefront in everything you do and work to impress him. We are here on earth because of God's grace so it is important that you stop and think what you have got, and where you have come from, but most importantly where you will go once you finish here. Thank Him for everything in your life. Thanking God should be done whole heartedly with meaning.

God always forgives what you have done. God does not look at the past, but he looks at today and where you are going. He does not judge what you have done before because he understands the negative power, the five negative forces and their effects on us as humans. We have to believe from the bottom of our heart that the creator of this universe is the provider for all.

God knows we are not perfect. He understands how the mind works and knows that we are chained to worldly pursuits and activities. There is a saying that every saint has a past and every sinner has a future. Today make that change and become the new saint who had a past but now has a great future.

When you were a soul in God's Kingdom of Heaven you asked the divine to come here on earth, promising that you will remember the Lord and to live by his commandments. Things like: earning an honest and clean living, doing good things for others, helping those in need, praying, living with integrity and not cheating and lying. You come on to earth as a baby and as you grow, the five forces become active and take over your life. The soul, the divine inside you gets overpowered and you soon forget the relationship you once had with God. So the divine being all love constantly reminds you by making things happen to you, making you feel isolated, making you feel alone, giving you health problems. He will send messages through others, but we just have to stop and pay attention because God knows it is when we are at our weakest we can be united with him.

Now for those of you that don't believe in God then you must learn to accept that there is a higher force: the energy that created this universe and keeps it going. That same energy has control of where you were born, who your parents are, how many brothers and sisters you have. This energy has some control over you and will create and give you things in life. This is the energy we need to thank and learn to love back as we live and go through our daily lives.

Another way to describe this is if you are living on earth without a physical mother or father then you can be at a slight disadvantage, not having the right tools and guidance to make decisions in life. Now the same principle applies to the divine, because without leaning on this power you can be at a great disadvantage. You have to remember that the divine is the creator of the universe and the creator of yourself. In order to be successful in life you need to lean on this power so you are able to achieve your full potential. The divine is always trying to guide you and tell you what direction to go in, but we suppress these thoughts and the mind pushes them down not allowing you to action the good deeds. If you can recall back to your childhood days, you would rely on your parents to provide and support you. Now we should be living our lives doing the same with the divine and watch how we reach our souls' purpose in life.

Chapter 3

Flow

"The doer of good rejoices here and hereafter; he rejoices in both the worlds. He rejoices and exults, recollecting his own pure deeds"
    (The Dhammapada, the Buddha's path to Wisdom 1:16)

In this chapter we cover several elements and we get to understand the term 'Flow'. This means to let things come to you naturally, and move from you naturally. This could mean giving things away to charity, giving your wealth away to the needy, your time, while equally accepting things that come into your life. What flows in must flow out and vice-versa. Allow no blockage in giving and accepting energy, time or money.

The first element we must let flow is time. We must give our time away selflessly. We must do things for others without expecting any reward. For example: helping a charity for three to four hours per week, or taking elderly people out on events, or walking the dog for someone who is no longer able. There are many forms of selfless service, but it is important we put effort into giving our time away. You will find that by giving your time away to others altruistically you will achieve what you want in a shorter time frame.

Now you might be thinking that you have so much going on in your life, it is too busy and hectic for you to give up three hours per week to help someone in need. This is exactly what people usually think. However, to realise the Gift, you need to go against the tide and get out of your comfort zone. I can guarantee that if you take your time to help those who need it, God will not leave you short of your destiny, in fact, quite the opposite; the positive energies you create and send out will come back to you; you will start seeing more opportunities coming up and things will start going your way more often. God will accelerate your destiny and get you there quicker. By doing selfless service you will also find that you still get your daily tasks done. For example, after you return from annual leave you will find there is some catching up to do, over 100 emails in your inbox and so many queries. But do you achieve anything less in your life by letting time flow towards the needed? The answer is no. The work will still get done and you will still achieve in life what you set out to do. In fact, by doing selfless service you will feel recharged, relaxed, and most importantly positive about yourself. This encouraging energy can be passed to others. By doing selfless service you will also feel wanted. It encourages you to do positive things in life.

Selfless service does not work if you simply say that when you get time you will go and help at the charity shop, or donate things to charity and clear the garage, because this way you will never find time. Finding selfless service is as difficult as finding a permanent job. It will not come easily to you. You need to go out and actively find it and once you are successful thank God for it, hold on to it, appreciate it and be grateful you have it. Being humble, thankful and grateful for helping others needs to also be embedded in your selfless service routine should be part of your life. You will see that you will not be disadvantaged but, as reiterated earlier, you will in fact achieve your goals in a shorter time frame. If you don't believe me, go and speak to individuals who are now retired and who have spared regular weekly hours donating their time to a specific place that needed it. I can guarantee you they will say they did not go short and achieved much more in life than they expected. Don't take my word for it. Do your own research, go and speak with people and experience this for yourself.

When you concentrate your efforts into selfless service you will find that the divine power will step in to carry out and organise your work, and ultimately your life, for you. The divine power is far better at doing your work than you will be and it will help you reach your targets and get you to where you need to be far quicker than doing it yourself. So give attention to helping others and let the divine work for you.

Also when you perform selfless service and you give to others you will find this will give you happiness. Contentment and satisfaction will come naturally to anyone who gives to others. You will come to discover that there is vicious cycle within our worldly activities: we are constantly seeking for more money, better relationships, etc. We create expectations of where and whom we want to be, what we want to have, and we are never satisfied and truly happy. One of the secrets behind happiness is to give to others.

The second most important form of flow is money. Most of us work very hard in earning our money so we don't want to give it away. We must let money flow like water. The more you let money flow outwards away from you, the more money flows inwards back to you. I can guarantee that if you speak to anyone who has wealth, they give money away to charity or any other causes. This is a fact in life and the sooner you accept it the sooner you can be on your way. The real objective is to give ten per cent of earnings away to charity. This may seem a lot at the beginning, however you can start small. Start by giving away ten pounds per month and then slowly build on it. I can guarantee you that the money given will not be missed. However, please remember that the smaller the amount you are giving then the smaller the amount you will receive back. Open your heart and give with abundance, don't hold back and you will see the flow of money return back to you.

Now you might be thinking that you can barely make ends meet by giving money away. Well, that is the exact habit we have to break. The objective of doing this is that if we help others in need, God will not leave you short, but again, quite the opposite. He will give you more than you need. However, giving money away should be regular and not a one off. Once again, you will find that you feel good about yourself, you will feel positive and be able to share this positive energy with others around you.

Now, if you really cannot afford to give any money away, rather than chasing worldly pursuits, concentrate your efforts on raising money for others and carry out regular events. For example: climbing, cycling for 40 miles or running for 15 miles. Something where you can be challenged while raising money for charity. Then you can donate this money to a cause you believe in.

The third element in this chapter is about energy and how to engage with people. Let positive energy flow outwards to others and you will see that positive actions will come back to you – the same law applies. For example, when you meet people pay them a compliment, give them a hug, say nice positive things to them. In return you will see positive energy start to flow back to you, making you a much happier person. Don't comment on other people and try not to say negative things. Don't talk to someone and speak badly about someone else, because all this creates negative energy. When you create this bad energy you will find that you start to attract negative energy back to you. The reverse to this is to stay positive and refrain from talking ill against others. If you create positive conversations you will attract positive energy back towards yourself.

Now, to do these three elements is not easy, and as I have mentioned earlier it is like working against the tide at first. But once you get used to this and include it in your lifestyle, then it becomes easier. To summarise: you must give your money away, 10% of your earnings; you must give your time selflessly to others who need it, on a daily and weekly basis; and lastly, say positive things to people in conversation and try not to comment badly about anyone. You will notice that by doing these three things, immediately you will see the difference. You will automatically start to feel very good and positive and with this positive energy you will not only be able to help others but it will also be very hard to knock you down.

The main outcome of fulfilling these three elements is that it brings more wealth to you, you will fulfil your goals quicker and positive things/opportunities will start to happen around you.

Chapter 4

Transparency

It is very important in life to be transparent. Imagine we were made out of glass and people could see straight through us. We should walk around with nothing to hide and with no hidden agenda. We should be totally clear and transparent like water.

The first step to this is to accept who you are and where you currently are. When you speak to someone and you exaggerate who you are or how much wealth you have, the person who you are talking to does not actually care. When you walk away from that person, they will not think twice about the conversation you just had and probably exaggerate it further when talking to a third person, giving a very wrong idea of who you are. You will be feeling guilty about the lies you just told. This creates blockages in your system and can stop you from developing yourself to your highest peaks.

We all go through bad times. Don't be ashamed to tell people where you are at and what you are going through. You never know, the person who you are talking to might be able to help you. Most of the time we are trying to paint a pretty picture to others. Stop and think why. Why are you trying to portray yourself as someone you are not? The sooner you can accept your position to yourself and to others then God is ready to move you on. There is no shame in telling people when you are at your lowest.

Transparency also means to be clear and fair, so we should not adopt one rule for some and better rules for others. Stand by your principles and have one set of rules for all people. For example: if you are a manager or boss at work and someone you like requests a day off outside the rules and you grant it; however if someone else asks you for the same request but because you don't have a close of a relationship with that person, you decline them. Keep yourself consistent, fair and clear so you have nothing to hide. Living this way, there can be no come backs and people won't talk badly against you behind your back. Live by your principles and if people don't like it then they are people you don't need in your life. I know this might sound harsh but by adopting this method you will attract people you can trust and more importantly people will be able to trust you because they know you are a fair and equal person.

By adopting this law you will grow a great reputation amongst others and eventually will become a respected man or woman within your local community, and more importantly a person that people can trust and rely upon when difficult situations arise.

Now to fully understand this you have to believe that there is a divine power and that this source is the truth and nothing but the truth. Obtaining full greatness can only be done by attaching ourselves to this source. However, this source will only be able to enter into a complete clean vessel, which means that at all times we must remain truthful and transparent to all. Psalm 106 "There is joy for those who deal justly with others and always do what is right."

To be transparent means to be honest, to tell the truth no matter if it will hurt someone. I understand that it is very difficult to tell the truth to everyone at all times, but let's take a closer look at why we lie. There are two reasons behind a lie. First we lie because we don't feel the person we are lying to will accept or handle the truth. Second we lie to impress others. Let's take the first one. We have a situation and then we make up a story because we think the person we are telling will not like the truth or will get angry, so we bend it, brush it under the carpet and don't say anything at all. It's not our duty to analyse the outcome of what the other person will say or do. Nine times out of ten we want to tell them but we are afraid, so we block telling the truth. Then comes the guilt. If we do this it causes blockages in our bodies. This can cause unnecessary strain and makes mediation more difficult. It stops the source entering into our bodies. Whether the person you are telling can handle it or not is really not down to you. They might shout, they might disown you, they might hit you, but that's not your negative karmic balance to take – it's theirs. You have to take responsibility for your own soul/energy and they have to take responsibility for their actions and soul/energy. Yes, it can be upsetting but it's better to take the pain now and be honest rather than let it be brushed under the carpet and be exposed later, which could turn out to be worse. The best way to lead your life is to be upfront and confront everything, leaving nothing unsaid or hidden. Once you have told the truth, you will have a sense of relief, calmness and feel a lot lighter. This is the position you need to be in for meditation and for the divine to enter in. You will also find that leading a life in this way will raise your consciousness to a higher level. Once you achieve this you are no longer playing at the field everyone else is at. You will start to feel invincible and that nothing can tear you down and your goals become very realistic. Also by leading a life in this manner you have nothing to hide so no one can touch you or say anything about you that is not of general knowledge already.

The second reason why we lie is to fit in or to impress others. In order for the divine source to come into a clean heart we have to accept who we are and where we are in life. It's not your job to paint a rosy picture of your life, it is your responsibility to accept where the energy source has put you. By lying you are deceiving others who are also connected to the energy source, so you move nowhere and you will find that you keep going around in circles. We need to break this habit and accept who and where we are in life. If people don't fit within our current boundaries or boxes, then let them walk away. Please don't bend yourself to fit within their box. If you are trying to put square pegs into round holes and they do not fit, then walk away from those people. If people do not accept you for who you are then don't force them and move on, because the divine source will find you others who you can interact with, who fit within your box, and more importantly relationships where you don't need to lie.

The more transparent you are then the more of the divine energy you can receive. Your body will become a pure vessel.

It's very hard for us to be transparent all the time and lead completely truthful lives. But if you make changes from today and start cleaning your soul and body from deceptions and lies, then you will see that the more you reduce them, the more you are letting the power in, allowing it to raise your consciousness and help you achieve your goals. If your life is ruled by 60% lies then you are allowing only 40% of the divine power to come in to you. It is essential that we are transparent at all times.

The main outcome of being transparent is allowing the divine energy source to come in. It also creates better meditation. You will feel lighter and happier knowing you are leading a life of complete truth. It causes no strain on your body, and no blockages, allowing your internal energy to flow positively and freely. This makes it easier to connect with the divine source. Overall, you will lead a cleaner, happier life and over time will become a respected person within your local community and friends.

Chapter 5

To Reduce the Amount of Outward Negative Actions

In life we have two balances. One is the balance of our bank account and the other is our karmic debt balance. Generally speaking our objective in life is to increase the pound notes in our bank balances. However, often we neglect or fail to look at the balance of our karmic debt.

The simple way to explain this concept is if you believe in the saying "what goes around comes around" or in the saying mentioned before "what you shall sow is what you shall reap".

We all undertake negative actions, which sometimes we just cannot avoid. However, our main objective should be to try to reduce the amount of negative actions we consciously do.

Another term for negative actions, often quoted in religious and holy books, is sinning. Now, we cannot live our lives without sinning as there are circumstances that we cannot control. For example, when we drive we will kill insects and flies; when we walk we may kill worms in the street; when we talk we may offend somebody; we occasionally tell a lie, we sometimes abuse people or we get angry. Sometimes sinning can be out of our control depending on the circumstances we are in, and that is why it is so important to concentrate on improving the balance, by reducing the amount of negative actions over which we do have influence. However, by doing meditation we can clear and reduce our karmic debt. By remembering God, acting by His rules and minimising wrongdoing, we can clear our sins. So it is always important to keep meditation in first place, before any worldly activities. Carrying out daily meditation is necessary because going to a place of worship is just not enough.

It is like having a bank account. Every time you perform a negative action, you debit, and every time you carry out a positive action you credit. The overall objective in life is to stay in credit at all times, to have a positive balance. When you are in credit, the divine power will start to develop an interest in you and boost you up, taking you closer to your objectives and allowing you to develop yourself as a positive person with an escalating positive karmic balance. Limits that were once beyond your reach will now be open doors for new opportunities. You need to understand that this cannot happen overnight or even in months. It can sometimes take years to get to this stage. The most important thing is you keep working towards it, remain positive and patient and your time will come.

Actions like killing, abusing, raping, talking ill of someone, commenting on others, violence, lying and cheating are negative. They reduce our balance and pull us backwards. You may read this and think that it isn't you, but if you eat meat then you are a part of a karmic chain which reduces your balance. For example, if I hire Fred and pay him £1000 to kill Tom, then who do you think takes on the karmic debt? It will be me and Fred, because I have paid him £1000 for something wrong to happen, and Fred committed the crime. In terms of karmic debt we are both responsible and the load for executing Tom goes on to both of our balances. The same principle applies with eating meat. If you pay the butcher £5 for a chicken, and the butcher consequently pays £3 to the farmer who executes the chicken then who takes on the karmic debt for killing the chicken? You do, the butcher does and the farmer does. You are all responsible for the execution of the chicken. Animals are also part of the divine and have souls just like you but they are in a different form, a lower species. There is no difference if I pay someone for killing a human being, a horse or a chicken, the same principles apply. "Knowing and renouncing severely and singly the actions against living beings, (…) – a wise man neither gives pain to these bodies, nor orders others to do so, nor assents to their doings." (Acharanga Sutra 1.7.5 – Jainism scripture)

Now you might argue that being a part of a karmic chain for killing chickens is not the same as killing a human being.

You are right. The karmic load is a lot smaller. However, you will soon come to realise that fifty chickens equate to the same karmic load as one human being. So ask yourself how many chickens you have eaten over the years and do your own calculations on your karmic load. The same principle applies.

Now you might feel that God has brought these creatures here on earth for us to eat and it is our duty to feed on them. That's OK to believe this but if you really want to accelerate in this life time then you need to take responsibility for your own karmic actions and do the best you can to create a positive account. Most spiritual people will tell you that eating meat does dent your karmic balance. God does give us free will to make our own minds up here on earth, and the choice is ultimately yours.

It is important that you try and reduce the amount of negative actions you undertake. It is important to keep constantly improving the balance by doing good deeds. This can be helping others in need, donating wealth, encouraging people, donating blood, commenting in a positive way about people, paying compliments, giving your time away selflessly with no hidden agenda and generally being a positive person around others. By creating these positive actions we are counteracting the negative ones. The overall objective is to undertake more positive actions than negative, thereby creating a positive karmic balance.

You will see over time that by creating a positive balance you will start to excel to heights beyond your imagination.

By creating a positive karmic balance you will automatically start to feel very positive around people and when bad situations arise you will be able to handle them a lot better. Another outcome of having a positive balance is that it helps to raise your consciousness to a higher level and, as stated in the previous chapter, allows you to see things in a different context.

Keeping a positive balance makes you calmer and more confident, and most importantly at peace with yourself. You won't get upset easily and you will be less worried about circumstances, because you know you have enough karmic wealth in the bank to handle any bumps in the road. This will enable you to have a rock solid foundation and when you are in this positive state of mind it is very hard for someone or something to knock you down.

You will have a sense of invincibility and you will feel that anything can be achieved. You will feel invincible because you are not creating bad actions, so no one has anything over you. However, when you reach this stage and success is coming to you fast, do not let pride or ego come in to play. Remember to give God the glory for all that has been achieved. Adopting all the laws of 'The Gift' makes you strong and allows you to hold on to what you have done so far. If you return to your old habits, you will find things can slowly fade away, and that you keep going around in the same circle once again.

Now most of us believe in reaping what we sow. This means if we plant apples we get apples and we plant oranges we get oranges. So if we plant bad deeds then we shall receive bad deeds back. So the less arguing, the less ill talking, less negative commenting we do about others, the less cheating, back stabbing and violence; the less of this we shall receive back. By reducing the amount of negative outward actions you will receive less negative inwards actions. Furthermore, by doing less negative actions you will not have that sense of guilt or depression which pulls us downwards. In this state we can accept divine energy and we are very responsive to it, allowing us to move to a higher level. This is a very simple law and one easy to understand. In conclusion, to realise God's full Gift we have to suppress and reduce the number of negative actions we carry out. You might be asking yourself how we know which are negative actions and which are positive actions. Generally speaking, those actions that need to be hidden or brushed under the carpet are negative actions. Those actions that can be shared and talked about are generally positive actions.

Chapter 6

To stay around positive souls

The sixth law to obtaining the Gift is to be around positive people. The reason for this is because when we are interacting with these types of people we feel better, happier and generally on top of the world. You will feel that anything can be achieved and this is the state you need to be in order to be elevated to your greatest heights.

We are like aeroplanes. There are four things a plane needs to take off: thrust, drag, lift and weight. Now let us say for example there are fifty people in your life. We have to firstly identify who in your life brings you down and makes you feel negative; in other words, who in your life are drags and bring weight to you. Then you have to identify who in your life thrusts you and lifts you. Now it is not just a simple case of eliminating the drags and the weights from your life because they might be close relatives or friends. So instead we apply the 80/20 rule. If you have recognised that five people of the fifty are positive, then we have to spend 80% of our time with those five people and 20% of our time with the rest of the forty five people who weigh you down and are a drag.

By doing this exercise and identifying the people that lift and thrust you, and spending more time with them, you will come to realise that you became more confident. Now as far as the other 45 people in your life are concerned, please do not ignore them, but live on the surface with them. Do not engage in deep conversations with them about your problems or share your plans and dreams, as you will find you walk away from it more drained, uninspired and they may even talk you out of something good. Talk politely and make conversation about anything but your life. Keep the time spent with them short and sweet.

Now it could be a case where you live with someone negative in your own home. Then the best solution is to say very little, let them do the talking and try to agree with them. Silence can be the best weapon. If you become argumentative you will find that this can be draining and will zap your energy for the bigger and better things in life. Sometimes it's good to let people win the argument at home because you have a life beyond this which they are unable to see, and is far greater than they can imagine.

So now we understand that in order to fulfil your true destiny we need to be spending time with positive people who will elevate you, boost you, encourage you, praise you, make you feel confident and support you with your dreams. The more time you spend around negative souls can impact or slow down your destiny, they can put you in a lower state of consensus which is not the state you need to be in to reach your full heights in life. It is important to evaluate your position and go through a clutter clearing exercise. 80% of time around the relationships that bring you positivity and 20% of your time with the ones that bring you negativity.

Now it is also very important as part of this exercise to find someone who you look up to or aspire to. They might not be in your life on a daily basis, but it is important to identify and find them, then meet with them once every two or three months. They might be a millionaire, a guru, an entrepreneur, a creator, whoever they are, identify them and make a connection through friends, associates, LinkedIn, using the internet or whatever tools possible. The reason why this is so important is because bringing these people into your life plants seeds into your higher consciousness, motivates you and makes you feel that where you want to be is very achievable. It makes it less challenging to reach your destiny. Spending time in company with the people you admire makes your destiny tangible and you will feel it is not such a hard task to overcome.

Going back to staying around positive souls, I am not saying that the negative people in your life are necessarily bad people; it's just that they don't create the right atmosphere for you; they don't bring the right energies for you. However, they too have a purpose in life and they will bring the right energies to someone else, but it's not you. The ones you have identified as being negative are not doing it intentionally. It is their nature, and they feel that they are saying the right thing. Their upbringing and their outlook in life is different from yours. Most importantly, don't let them lead you astray.

Now you might think this law is harsh but the greatest Gift that God has given us is love. It is important that we feel in a positive state of mind by choosing the people we spend most of our time with so we are in a position to share our love and joy with others. The greatest Gift we can give back to the divine is to love his people.

After reading this you might reflect and find that you don't have anyone positive in your life who can encourage, praise and compliment you. That's OK. We are at a new beginning, so let's go out and find those people and invite them into our lives. Start to go to breakfast meetings, social events, gym classes, networking events, anywhere you are able to meet new faces. Don't be afraid of approaching new people. I can guarantee that if you say hello to someone, nine times out of ten they will say hello back and before you know it you could be in a full blown conversation. It is important to bring new people into our lives, bringing a fresh new outlook. New faces mean new innovation.

Starting today, analyse the people around you, and use the 80/20 rule, spending most of your time around the positive souls. Invite new faces into your life and spend less time with people who have a negative approach towards you. This can be a long drawn out process, but it is important to do this because you will not be able to fly high if there is too much drag and weight around you. Change your life today and put this into action, surrounding yourself with those souls who will lift and thrust you. You will then begin to see yourself towering to top altitudes.

Chapter 7

To be pure of heart

To be pure of heart means to be in a state where you are listening to your heart and not your mind. To lead a life ruled by your heart means to lead the life of love. All actions you take should be genuine and not false. To be clean of heart you need to open it to everyone, to love everyone, to help everyone, to not lead anyone astray, or to have any ulterior motives or any hidden agenda. Following the heart means following the divine and the Gift will only work if all seven laws are carried out with full heart.

Now you might find that if you lead a life full of love and follow the heart then you could be hurt easily. This is true, if you follow this law alone, which is why you must use all seven laws together. For example, meditation allows you to detach yourself from people and objects so that when relationships break or you lose things or even loved ones, it softens the blow so and don't lose your balance. Listening to the heart is like actioning the higher consensus. Going further, it is like listening to the divine power that created you and this universe. If you listen to it, you can never go wrong, because all actions undertaken will be carried out of love, which is in fact the way God wants us to live our lives – based on love. A lot of you currently have the ability to listen to this voice inside but you are so used to keeping it suppressed and half of the time you don't action the thoughts.

Imagine you are in a restaurant and you ask for the bill. The waiter gives you the wrong bill by mistake and charges you for the next table. Two things can happen here, either the bill is considerably larger than it should be, which instantly makes you bring the mistake to the waiter's attention; or the bill is relatively smaller. If the former happens, then similarly you will want to tell the waiter straightaway, however if we do not have a pure heart or are working towards having one, the negative forces will kick in and undermine your initial instinct – i.e. greed. You will stop for a second and think: 'I could use this extra money; it wasn't even my mistake…' etc. Listen to your heart in every situation, before your mind and the forces come into action, and make a decision based on your heart. By doing this, you will not create a chain of negative actions that will eventually come back to you; the waiter won't be in trouble for the mistake, he will actually be grateful towards you and treat you well next time you come.

It is difficult to stay on this path of the heart, but I can guarantee that you will lead a better life. Often the heart will tell you to do the right things but then very quickly you will be powered by the five negative forces pushing that good thought down. To bring the heart out you need to stop suppressing it and start to action it. Start with small steps. It will be difficult at first, but then you will become better at it and before you know it, you will be leading a life led by love. For example, if your heart tells you to go and help someone, don't look around to see what others are doing, just go on and help them. If your heart tells you to see someone that is feeling low, then don't go and analyse what others are doing and judge what they have done, just go and see them and make them feel better. The heart is all clean. By following your heart you will always do the right actions and lead a much better life. You will find that you will be doing a lot more positive actions which can be reaped later in life.

Being pure of heart means being in state where you are listening to your heart and immediately actioning it without waiting for another force to come into play to stop it. However, you must do what the heart is comfortable with. For example, if you are doing selfless service and you are forcing ten hours a day and it does not sit well with you, reduce the hours to something you are comfortable with. Or if you are doing selfless service and it does not feel comfortable because you don't like the people or atmosphere, then find another selfless service you can do. It does not make a difference how much or what selfless service you do, just make sure you are happy and enjoy the service.

If your heart tells you to stay away from someone or to move jobs then listen to it, do not suppress it. If you are doing things with your heart then it means you are doing it with full love, and something you are doing with full love means you have the divine behind you. You will ultimately be successful in it, whether it is relationships, work or selfless service.

You can see that the true self is all heart and love. For example, when you go out and drink you will find that it can temporarily block the five forces, greed, lust, pride, attachment and anger. You will find yourself having a good time, being joyful and relaxed, and most importantly loving towards others. This is because alcohol lowers our inhibitions and blocks the five senses. This is the person who wants to enjoy life, who wants to have a great time. The inner you, the one who lives for the moment isn't worried about what happens tomorrow. This is how God wants us to live our lives. However, we cannot get into the habit of drinking because it is an addiction and most importantly it is not good for the body. Excessive amounts leads to other things like violence. Instead we should learn to meditate to block these five downward forces. This will give you the same intoxication feeling and help you access the divine.

To realise the Gift we have to thank God for all that happens in our life. The secret behind this is not just to thank God in a routinely manner on Sundays or grace before dinner but to thank God from the bottom of your heart at all times and to mean it. You have to surrender to God and eventually to be in a state where you feel he is in control of everything in your life. Whatever happens in your destiny, whether you perceive it to be good or bad, you must thank the divine. This needs to be done with full heart and clean intentions, not choosing to thank God when it suits you. In the bible it states, "blessed are the pure in heart for they will see God." I cannot stress enough that in order to realise the Gift you need to fully trust in the divine and be thankful. It is only then you will come to realise and see the true potential of the relationship we can have with God and where he can take you.

This is God's world. He is the creator of the universe and it is by the grace of God that we are here. So we have been given this rare opportunity to come here on to earth and we should not take our lives for granted. We need to realise that this chance will not come again soon. So we need to thank that divine energy from the bottom of our heart and really mean it. Once we are truly and sincerely thankful, then the divine energy will elevate you to the highest planes.

Let's take downloading free music online as an example. Now your mind tells you that you don't want to pay for a track from iTunes or the local record store. Greed comes into play and you find a way of downloading the music for free. However, your heart knows this is the wrong thing to do, but you continue to do it. Put yourself in the artist's shoes. One day you write a book, record a song or make an innovative piece of work or even a product. How would you feel if someone else stole the idea, your work or your master piece? You would feel miserable, hurt, disappointed and quite low. This is how artists feel and yet every day millions of people in the world are doing this. Then we ask ourselves why we are not gifted? Why are we not where we should be? Why have we not got wealth? Why are we not happy? The divine power will not elevate you if you are not listening to it. Buying an artist's song from iTunes is the same price as buying a pint of milk, if not less. Is it really worth cheating the artist for that little money? You do more harm to yourself by doing this than the artist. To have a relationship with the divine is a two way street. To live a life led by the divine is to follow what your heart tells you to do. How can the divine elevate you if you doing wrong to others? Give the artist the recognition they deserve and buy the song legitimately through the appropriate channels. Remember, what goes around comes around.

So it is important to live a life led by your heart and action what the higher consensus is saying to you. Don't suppress the thoughts because it is the easiest thing to do. You need to ride against the tide and realise the full potential of your gift. You need to carry out meditation, and thank God for everything that happens in your life. The most important ingredient in realising the full potential of your gift is to live a life of hearts. Only those who are clean of heart will have success in love and life, peace, happiness and wealth and will have a true relationship with the divine power, the creator of the universe, who is the provider of all great things in your life, the one who will take you to your true heights so you don't just keep going around in the same circles.

Action Plan

Now that you have read the book it is important to draw up an action plan and start to adopt the gift into your life. Today you can make the change if you so desire and lead a life that will take you to your highest destiny.

What you need to do is to concentrate your life and actions towards the seven laws and you will find that the worldly activities will take care of themselves.

The actions we make today will determine what happens tomorrow. For example, today you are confronted with someone who is angry. You have the choice to be angry back and argue, the choice to hit, abuse or kill, or you have the choice to go against the tide, smile and walk away. However, the choice is yours. Whatever you decide today will impact tomorrow. If you choose to walk away then perhaps after things calm down you can speak again to each other tomorrow. If you decide to have a full on argument, then perhaps you won't speak to each other for a week or so. If you chose to hit or kill, then the police will turn up on your doorstep tomorrow arresting you for murder. Today we are living a life of the seeds already planted and today we have free will to plant new seeds of greatness which will impact our futures.

It does not make a difference what seeds you have planted in the past but today you can start afresh and draw a line under what has happened previously. Plant seeds of greatness and change your destiny. The divine power is all love, and created you out of love. He is all forgiving and wants you to excel to your greatest heights. However, the divine power is all fair, it cannot be cheated and it doesn't give you shortcuts. It can only elevate you if you are in the right state of mind, through the right channels, so make the changes you need to make today and take control of your life. Watch how by using 'The Gift' you can be taken to your full potential and fulfil what the divine power has brought you here on earth to do.

Today has been decided by previous actions you have taken. Today you will create new actions that will determine your destiny in the future. You are in control of your own life and it is down to the actions that you undertake as to where you can reach in this life time.

Working towards the gift is to say we are improving our karmic balance in our bank account. We need to work towards achieving a positive balance; as a result we will have optimistic outcomes in the physical world we live in. The problem with us all is that we concentrate too hard on worldly activities to improve our lives. For example you don't need to chase loved ones, work twelve hours a day, work every day, chase money or be insecure. To improve our situation in our life rather than concentrating on the issue, instead we need to focus our attention on increasing our karmic balance through using the seven laws. Automatically things that you desire will start to appear in the physical world.

Draw a new line today, change your life and make the necessary actions. Start by looking for selfless service. You may not need to look far but even in your own work place. There are always people struggling with their workloads or sales. Take time out and help, develop and coach them. This is selfless service. By spending time with colleagues who need your help you will find that you will not go short in your own destiny, or work that you need to carry out yourself. However this service needs to come from the heart and you must have the desire to help with no hidden agenda, you need to do this while being pure of heart.

In order to measure your success in life you need to measure how much of the gift you are using. So don't look at the balance in your bank account, or the fact that you want a baby, or a house or a better car. Ask yourself how much time a day you give for meditation? How much are you thanking God for what happens in your life? How much time do you spend selflessly for others? How transparent are you? Are you keeping your karmic actions to a minimum? Do you love everyone that the divine power has put in your life or do you have jealous thoughts? Are you always comparing their material possessions with your own? The more you get hung up about others, the less the divine power will not aid you in achieving what you desire in your world. You should be happy for others and this joy should not be false, it should come from the heart. Ask yourself if you are using these seven laws to their full potential. If not then work towards them and give it 150%. Watch over time how you will start to achieve your wishes and desires.

Begin to make an action plan and start with the first law, meditation. The ultimate goal is to achieve around two and a half hours per day. That might sound like a lot, but it's just 10% of your time per day. However, let's start small with around five to ten minutes per day and gradually grow it. This is a marathon, a new way of life. It cannot be a short burst of sprinting because like a rocket you will shoot up but come crashing straight down. Take your time, be patient and the results will come.

Second, find a cause you believe in and start to make small donations on a monthly basis. Find a charity you feel passionate about where you actually want to see a difference. This could be a small local charity or a large national or international one. The choice is yours. You should do it with your heart. You should want to make cut backs on your spending, i.e. takeout food, shopping, clothes, whatever; anything you can save on the side should be donated to the charitable cause you are supporting.

The next step is to find somewhere you can give your time away. As mentioned earlier, this could be like finding a permanent job and is not easy. However, start at work and help others around. Or find something else like a charity shop, local hospices, churches, temples, places of worship, anywhere where they need help. As you begin to use the GIFT your success will start to climb and selfless service will help you stay grounded and stay positive.

When good things happen in your life, thank the divine from the bottom of your heart. Start today, begin by saying thanks for getting me to work safely, thank you for that sale, thank you for the car, thank you for the new house, thank you for the new business, thank you for letting me meet that person and thank you for a great day. However, these thanks must come from the heart and you must sincerely mean it. You need to actually feel that the divine power is doing everything for you and to appreciate everything that comes into your life. The more you become grateful towards the power then the more grace it gives you. In other words, the further you lean towards the divine then the more it becomes a part of your everyday life and pushes you further in your destiny.

Start to analyse yourself and find out what you are hiding. Whatever it is, come clean. Don't hide anything. Become fair and transparent; don't do any actions in secret. Become an open book. Don't do any actions where you feel ashamed by doing them. Don't do any actions behind someone's back. And slowly watch how all your blockages leave your system. By doing this action you are cleaning your mind and soul and allowing the divine to come in to raise you to high altitudes. Without this cleansing process it is very hard to move on.

Write on a piece paper all the people you see on a daily or monthly basis. Highlight the ones that make you feel positive, joyful, optimistic, and upbeat and make a point to spend more time with them. The ones that make you feel low and drag you down, don't interact with them as much and keep those relationships on the surface.

And finally from today onwards start to reduce the amount of negative actions you undertake. Don't hurt anyone, don't hit anyone, don't abuse anyone, don't ill comment on anyone and finally try not to be a part of any karmic chains that relate to a death of any soul on earth.

I can guarantee you that if you go and speak to someone who has success in wealth they will be pushing flow hard. Go and speak to someone who has happiness in relationships and you will find they are very transparent. Speak to someone who is constantly at peace and has sanity, and they will be carrying out a lot of meditation. Speak to someone who has happiness in their life and you will find they are staying around positive souls. I can guarantee that if you speak to someone who has overall success in their life, you will find they are keeping their negative outward actions to a minimum. So people who have success in relationships, wealth, love and happiness are pushing the seven laws hard. Using the Gift has become a way of living for them. They will not tell you this, but if they have success in one of those areas they are pushing that particular law of the 'The Gift'.

In conclusion, meditation gives you peace and contentment, giving God the glory gives you humility and allows you to stay humble in life. Flow gives you wealth, transparency gives you success in relationships and staying around positive souls keeps you happy. Reducing the amount of negative outward actions allows the divine to elevate you to your greatest altitudes. Being pure of heart allows you to have a relationship with the divine and to always have the divine power behind you. Overall, working towards THE GIFT gives you peace, success in relationships, wealth, love, happiness and most importantly allows one to reach their true destiny without having to chase it.

However, the choice is yours. This is not something we can do for several weeks or months and then give up. This has to be your lifestyle. It will take around eighteen months minimum before you start to see the results you want. You must be patient and be able to enjoy the new lifestyle.

You must appreciate this GIFT given to you by the Almighty, and use the time you have in this life wisely. Work towards the seven laws and return this GIFT back to the divine. The choice is yours to implement the GIFT today and see where it takes you.

However, the most important thing you must do alongside the seven laws is constantly drive and push the boundaries over. If you exercise the seven laws without the drive and determination to succeed then nothing will happen. You always need to put in all your efforts in relationships, marriage, work, business and whatever you want to achieve in life. This, along with the seven laws, will bring you the results you want. Now you might be thinking that you always put 150% effort into everything you do, but seem to be going nowhere. Effort and determination with the seven laws go hand in hand. Once you learn this you will see that you will be elevated to heights beyond your beliefs.

Summary

Applying 'The Gift'

Whether you are a sportsman, businessman, manager, director or employee you can use 'The Gift'. Apply 'The Gift' and it works on anything you do, whether you want success in business, relationships or love, it works in all areas.